REGARD THIS AS EVIDENCE

LAMBSKI

authorHOUSE®

AuthorHouse™ UK
1663 Liberty Drive
Bloomington, IN 47403 USA
www.authorhouse.co.uk
Phone: 0800 047 8203 (Domestic TFN)
+44 1908 723714 (International)

Published by AuthorHouse 10/29/2019

ISBN: 978-1-7283-9476-3 (sc)
ISBN: 978-1-7283-9475-6 (e)

Print information available on the last page.

This book is printed on acid-free paper.

Foreword

When slaves revolt they don't care if they die because all life is only death, in every breath the taunts of power for slavery is the birth of power and power was built on slavery. The boundaries of capital are burned for a race of thieves to unite beneath flags coloured with the blood of victims for the glory of power. The power only exists to control for abuse, the victims are slaves the dispossessed, those driven from their Homes by laws by war by lies of freedom that only enslave with the morality of murder and the justification of ruler ship by men whose very acts of democracy were conjured up by illusions funded by theft.

What is it then when a slave dies? What is the loss? The loss of free labour, profit and control. What laws protect the enslaved against death whilst they are guzzled with the religions of hypocrisy. The religions of hypocrisy that created slavery to build capitalism.

So now the capitalism of our sustained lives enslaves us with the economies of the system. That not only destroys labour but now also the earth with indifference to it's life and worth. The air we breathe. Nature will spew her anger into the face of tyranny that rules the earth by war by class and economic slavery. And so the tyrants can drink oil at the feast of their re-birth to golds power to destroy, and me another slave to die? Well I'll always be.... Lambski

Dedicated to Pam

Anger

The anger of a nation,
and a spark to light it's flame.
The mounted force of order,
charges once again.
I watch and see with horror,
the weapon of the state.
Take it's wage of blood and tears,
from those who demonstrate.

The cries of defiance,
are shouting loud and clear.
The well of my emotion,
becomes an outraged tear.
In the centre of democracy,
the power tends not to see.
The chant of a protestor sings,
that we are proclaimed free.

Kings and Governors

Dawns of requirement begin without trust,
Corroding the bullion with lies into rust.
Launching uranium into wealth's stolen sky,
Asking the weatherman if it's raining and why.

Oh I know truth has become real,
From my treasures liars steal.
To hoard deceits throne of greed,
And say through teeth that you are freed.

Did you see newsday spawn the lie?
Dressed up like monarchy refusing to die.
Justifying slaughter like it was a gift,
Giving another hate crime excuse in the twist.

Why can't freedom mean the word?
Why can't victory be the first?
How is it that your chains are gold?
When it was all lies you ever told.

Was it just a cooling breeze?
That brought me ever to my knees.
Before my love stirred tears to burn,
Into your face where passions learn.

When was the season of their Reich?
Smashing down my favourite strike.
Across the fields of where we live,
And now they ban me to forgive.

Walk Every Mile

Breaking apart your skies for a vision,
Leaning toward the new found decision.
To fight for the air we need for our lungs,
And combat the sunrays of eternal new suns.

Newsday interrupts the truth everyday,
Churches poison the pulpits if you dare there to pray.
Listen to music to throw every shape,
Watch as corruption inflicts earth with rape.

Climate is changing to stop it comply,
Pollution now rampant brings raintown to cry.
Wasted revulsion records every drop,
Flooding the media who grow hate for crop.

Smoking in unison a high to forgive,
Crimes over poverty now too poor to live.
Streets empty quickly shops are shut down,
Beggars for glory now ruling the town.

Visual remnants of broken up vessels,
In times recoiling away through springtime in petals.
Left wondering awaited for annoyed despair,
Queuing up lonely for moral repair.

Torn orders flake like snow in dark winter,
Frozen deals reminisce ignoring the sprinter.
Across your drifted snow plain of a stolen dream,
Feeding your face like a rabid obscene.

Where were you, you brothers in streets full of blood,
Bearing your meaning to anoint for above.
You never saw moonbeams pleading with stars,
You lost what you came for to burn my regards.

We May Not Care

Highways of the mind,
lost on planet kind.
To touch another heart in song,
floating through a tasty bong.
Where never was as never said,
each heart we turn to kiss is bled.
When noise becomes a beauty scene,
in a cold and darkened dream.
For this love we tread the stair,
with blood upon it slashed so rare.
Because blood never reasons why,
beneath the clotted cloudy sky.
Of why we rant and spew the word,
to those who defy the tune we heard.
Denying all the moist debate,
tuning into the show too late.
Whilst love could hurt the virgin heart,
waiting for the new dawns start.
Where lost inside the newly kissed,
are heartbeats that our love had missed.
For learning hurt the young may cry,
as all the old will turn and die.
When youth becomes a shining blade,
in all this burning blood red rage.
To waste where futures call becomes,
living in these darkened slums.
Where hope burns the coloured vote,
as Obama drums the changing note.
Because the rain soaked earth is where,
we bleed to know we may not care.

Cliffs of Dover

You are so lovely like flowers in the sun,
like daydreaming of your embrace and kisses.
Oh like nothings real except you.
All the others fade away,
I feel so lonely in this world of blue.
Touch me make me shiver,
make me warm so cold I am.
Bless your eyes and your heart,
I worship this feeling,
I know I am dreaming.
Could you ever be mine?.
Hurting bad my heart beats painfully,
when you are close I feel such a fool,
to have this emotion for you.
Poets dream away on clouds,
poets cry of love unfound.
These yearning words need your kiss,
how can all life come to this.
In times of lonely minutes past,
to hours without you sweetest love.
But your hearts for another,
with kisses for your lucky lover.
I'm sorry everything feels empty,
I'm poor and lost tattered and free.
This love I have is flying over,
my English Rose,
the cliffs of Dover.

Summer Storm

Dissolution of impact,
strained in tears on untouched eyes.
Broken to pieces over ranting bones,
squealing in motion of rotating lies.

Gathered up beside a lost road,
repenting over desired sensation.
Repeating guesses in a circle,
going around and around a nation.

Notoriety becomes abnormal,
because ideas torch reasons touch.
Levelled out by another bomb blast,
as peace becomes a move too much.

Never opting for the sundown,
regretting sunrays burn again.
Kissing limbs with carefree dances,
emotion reels beneath the pain.

Dividing light from darkness,
moonbeams creep in shadows drawn.
Now becoming lost at midnight,
blackness brews a summer storm.

Burn in You

Souls dissolve in corrosive lies,
blankly touching blind mans eyes.
In the matter of hypocracies faint smile,
crawling through syringes pile.
Never catching enlightened space,
a clearing for some sane new taste.
Bought for by new rules for flight,
darkened in a quest through night.
Where evil taunts recount deception,
elected by a blank led nation.
Forgetting births rejoicing entrance,
into calamities sinful credence.
Where logic retains the golden goal,
to follow home a trained new soul.
Lost between choice so stark,
biting bullets to cough and bark.
An order for revealed true love,
without consigned surges of blood.
As gifts become a plea for truth,
corrosive lies that burn in you.

The Daughters of Rebbecca

Through a cloud of stormy weather,
came the Daughters of Rebbecca.
With blackened faces like welsh coal,
burning the gates that charge the toll.

Ragged starving marching men,
anger inflamed at rising rent.
With children dying on their feet,
in the slums of a dead end street.

Carmarthen people worked so hard,
to send the coal and steel abroad.
Across the oceans of stinging sweat,
to feed an empire of the bled.

Petticoats so white and torn,
everyman for death was sworn.
The martyrs of a bloody battle,
refusing to die docile like cattle.

Raped the country of the song,
that dragon slept and did no wrong.
Oh the profits went to London town,
and we would dream to burn it down.

A humble choir turns me to tears,
a hymn of passion sung for years.
Would wake Rebbecca's ghosts to roam,
her daughters now are marching home.

The Scar of McGilligan

Comrades, I would like to get a job,
and if I don't you will only be left in doubt.
About that howling hurricane,
that sought to drive the wind and rain,
into the hostile Salisbury plain.
So if I manage on my knees,
my wages will be the sins for what they say in collusion
with their own liberties.
Behind the vision of a new century,
but what's the use of all thats free to the salutations of
conception to the plough,
we drive the hardest bargain in the clouds of chairman Mao.

Considering devices to maintain the liberation of the
blackest hearts amongst us,
that want to shout the words triumphant, Oh Hallelujia
come my way.
The greatest day of freedom in the tears we sow to gain the
heart to say we need them,
and not the choice they give away.
More blood has gained momentum inside a heart that beats
inside
me crying out for victory.
And on the TV screen before me I saw a man who'd got
his gutsfill
let the words just float around him,
as he blended his intrusion,
into the bloody revolution.

Refugee

Without any reason we walk through the rain,
in silence that says more than the words I have wrote.
Today I am feeling real small like an ant,
with no voice with no home and no vote.

Behind me in ruins lies the city we built,
to this evening I cannot raise a smile.
It is what we thought would always remain,
but my home is now heaped in a pile.

I fall into the mud and nobodies arms help me free,
and I am crawling along through my land.
Ahead is the river that I'll swim in retreat,
for I have not one comrade to stand.

The terror machines of war are riotous,
the display in the night sky is too real.
For peace will not come to the factions at large,
as they clash to declare a conflicting ideal.

I am a refugee,
no leader will listen to me.
I must run for my life and never look back,
I must care for my wife and find a safe track.
I have no colours and no values remain,
should I carry on walking through this god awful rain?.

Look at my city burn in the night,
look at the people who are not in the fight.
Listen and hear the last cries of my child,
caught by a bullet that strayed and went wild.
This war creates another reason for more,
in this war.

Love Hearts

Especially in the summer does my heart recall you fairly,
for the splendour of your cultivated beauty I believed
so much in your love to spare me.
Spare me from the rejection of an autumns dulcet enticement,
away into new arms,
new eyes to see your beauty.
For those who yearn for melody,
for those who instruct jealousy.

My own heart albeit arrogant,
does recall the equal knave.
Yet it is not in wonder that I may lose you,
for another heart that you may save.

For now recovering from the first bites of your cobra love,
I have seen your weakness in nights of joviality.
Now on a level par you come again to me and talk of love,
in whispered tones of impartiality.

Come then dearest to my touch,
forget the others who now forgo any recall of even your hairs
beauty,
they in jealous banter forstall the initial emotion of our
truth.
You see it is envious,
it is malice.
Oh but your heart is stained not so much,
and I hold your passion in my chalice.

Then no fear between us can belie our insidious tears of woe
to those who may corrupt our watery repose.
And I declare as if I have championed your heart, oh fair and
dearest.
Let us leave the gossip to a lesser mans denial.

That you my belle are radiantly gorgeous,
oh my heart does swell.
Here beside me your bosom heaves,
your heart believes,
my love is true.
Only to you in this evening times appraisal.

Beating True

Catch my smile upon your lips,
In the fields of morning mist,
Where life becomes another day,
To twist and turn the tears away.
like dancing rays of dawns elite,
in true designs of the sun complete.

Through the sleeping towns of England breath,
Where love grows cold and prides bereft.
Of the will to stand and sing the song,
When youths unite to smoke the bong.
And waste their visions in the smoke,
Where once our bravest were awoke.

To tunes of valour blood and tear,
A land that laughed and spat at fear.
Then raised it's fist to justify,
Refusing to retreat through hail and die.
And be destroyed like victims do,
Because of the heart that pounds in you.

Love Beach Blues

Sitting down to reason things together,
it's hard to gather what you have not got.
But what is it that makes you wonder?,
when you are sat upon the lot.

Looking around my eyes were dazzling,
I caught her eye to last a stare.
I watched for hours as she lay dreaming,
in the sunshine we had to share.

My thoughts went gliding down her shoulders,
across her rib cage to her hips.
And as the sun made her much more browner,
I almost crawled the beach to kiss her lips.

Sensation now the memories here again,
a warm feeling giving me all her blues.
I could cry now if I watched her leave once more,
last time she dressed I got the news.

That was only hours ago at 3pm,
and this evening I curse away each cloud.
I don't want them gathering tomorrow,
lets see the sun beat strong and proud.

I worship the sun as it sets toward the ocean,
there was a flower today it brought to bloom.
I want to find out her name so badly,
I want her passion in my room.

Give me your love oh sweetest angel,
but this rhyme you'll never see.
Unchain me from the shackles of this memory,
the loves inside my heart to set us free.

Divinity

When divinity retires this morn',
will you still require your scorn.
In quietness I have come to reason,
disdain acquires no particular season.
For in time the singing truth will quarry,
all your pockets filled with sorry.
Though may my eyes be blessed with splendour,
in summer days that well remember.
Your beating heart that tires not ill,
your loving touch that came to kill.
All my hope for our tomorrow,
when dignity was on the borrow.
Though muddy fields became my home,
I was not born to cry and roam.
These green plush hills of passions flower,
addicted to the summer shower.
Where dance rainbows for hidden gold,
more precious than the love we sold.
That day was long and tears renewed,
the crying humble multitude.
In hours now lost to crazy ramble,
to ask for love was such a gamble.
And though I thought my beauty pleasant,
I lost my way in heartaches desert.
All was lost till feathers chirping,
talked of adventures with so much loving.
Oh so wonderful is summers reign,
that I'll not travel lost again.
Because this growling empty chasm,
is not here for me to fathom.

Maze

Searching in a maze of forgotten dreams,
I pass beyond the realm of fantasy scenes.
To find the eloquence of a nurtured treasure,
heart beating loudly with a taste for pleasure.
Lost for a thousand years in secret hiding,
like a golden cache of love worth finding.
Is your love so serene and pleasant,
remarkable words would seem so flippant.
When the key to loves joy are a flurry of kisses,
delayed for your smile beats my heart into misses.
Catching my breath that is stolen away,
on the breeze of flirtation of a sunshiney day.
Like the heavenly touch of a sweet smiling angel,
like the secret of love that no mortal can tell.
'Neath the quaint avenue of a clouds passing shape,
the fluffy white mass of a rainbursts escape.
Oh on invisible wings your smile captures the words,
that are trapped on my tongue that the knowledge deters.
For your dangerous heart sets the vision into skies,
that cannot be captured nor caught by surprise.
Where freedom does breed on eternities wings,
where the free flying bird writes the songs that he sings.
For tomorrow we feast on the day that has passed,
to be hungry no more and never more do we fast.
An abundance of joy rains down from the storm,
which passes too briefly with all it's grumbling to warn.
There is talk in the hillsides that love will not die,
and all the tears that are falling will be wiped away dry.

The Peoples Turn

Wherever I look I see desolation,
in this and every other nation.
Discarded syringe from someones high,
babies, children, mothers die.
Bullets and bombs for someones cause,
corpses rot to the butchers applause.
Countries torn by new invasion,
arm the children for deprivation.
Destroying love the wars roll on,
the protest singer sings no song.
Silence grips the tongues of peace,
the revrend prays for war to ceace.
Churches are empty and the mosques burned down,
refugees in droves leave town.
Deserted streets napalmed to dust,
America say's in God we trust.
Those dollars pay me smack tonight,
coz when I'm high the clouds real tight.
The rain has stopped and the sun comes to see,
if a new day sets the people free.
Chains of commerce pay by the hour,
money is the new world power.
In the press the deals been done,
now we all wait for Christ the Son.
Who sits at home and cries his tears,
evicted soon for rent arrears.
The streets are ugly the whole world over,
paranoid eyes from New York to Dover.
The Statue of Liberty signs on for welfare,

her burning torch now needs repair.
One world one peace to last forever,
no leaders and no stormy weather.
Utopia defies the profit of fools gold,
no more guns and death are sold.
Rainbows rise to greet the dawn,
now the paths to peace are worn.
And singing breezes whisper love,
our leader is the sacred dove.
Tonight the stadium is full,
tonight flowers are on the pull.
And moonbeams bless the ocean clean,
oh please don't wake me from this dream.
For honey and milk from Mr King,
can bring me all my freedom, sing.
Sing with me a song today,
call a tune from pipers gay.
Across the world unite and cry no more,
for what is all the hatred for.
For skin colour for borders for religion,
for some liar or polotician.
Whose idea destroys deception,
truth cries out without connection.
The oceans are deep the depths are cold,
so what does the future hold.
Surely not more hate and war,
the lust for blood for more more more.
Machines of hate harvest the crop,
until they collect blood, oh every drop.

The earth is stained forever now,
if we fail peace without renown.
Will they end it all with nukes today,
by whose right I bloody say.
The earth is our only sacred home,
it's where all generations have been sown.
They're shitting in my garden,
the stench is getting harder.
How long can we breath the air polluted,
now that the rain forests being looted.
Wealth is all that has been regarded,
from my heart all hopes departed.
A bunch of bastard profiteers,
rule the earth without their ears.
The system is out of control,
and we lost count of what they stole.
For we were blind and thought unclean,
with no invites to the richmans dream.
Too far too long we are too quiet,
frustration comes and so we riot.
Burn the banks and institutions,
shoot the rich just like the Russians.
But then we are soiled with tainted blood,
after crawling through their stinking mud.
Oh go home and cry forever,
the system is complex and clever.
We have no weapons but do we need them,
when the swords no match for liberties pen.
Unity, unity in some land somewhere.

people loving to breath clean air.
Washed clean by their faith and hope,
with hearts for love that now can cope.
I need this land just like a passion,
the earth will see love in fashion.
Economic rule collapse and burn,
for now it is the peoples turn.
International, international world revolving,
who wants the job of problem solving.

Suss the Ghanja Riot

Calling the intrepid desire to locate within the definition
of retaliation,
Weighed deeply was an anchor of summers mellow forgiveness
in a plume of
ghanjas emancipation.
I and I alone found the movement of rebellious cloud,
It was for the hesitant horizon held in the last hours of a
misty shroud.

The streets held an uneasy calmness almost empty save the
odd passing car,
A man black dressed in colours walked accompanied, Rasta.
At the end of the road a police van stationary locked in tension,
Broken bottles and crumbling bricks purvey evidence of the
nights extension.

Smouldering shop fronts and shattered glass broken
consumerism recalls,
The anger ignited with fury for the revelation of peace that
stalls.
Shouts of anger pours fire growling through the summer air,
And the pretence of order in the streets we scare.

With sweaty palms the molotovs grasped,
A stench of fear in the burns surpassed.
Defiant customs revolve within anothers mind,
As denigration resisted the laws unkind.
Like whispy rebels disappear into the night,
To clash and to prepare to fight.

Condemned by written compulsive lies,
Of political weathermen who's rain denies.

Crushed in spirit devolved to fate,
The building represents it's smoke till late.
When dawn became our accusing smile,
Convicted with our clothes in style.
Then to decide like lost cold begotten,
For anger left to spoil the nation rotten.
In corridors of corruption bleat,
A stained democracy in the street.

Light the Stars

Don't leave me now,
like petals falling from a flower.
Like the passing summer sunshine,
in a world of emptyness I wander.
stealing love like it's a crime.
A pleasant smile ignites my heart,
the early morn' is all I wanted.
To touch you when we are apart,
today forever we are bonded.
Forget the road where I was lost,
in a country prone to wasteland.
I found you a place without a cost,
with my soul now free to stand.
Come with me to the forest drove,
lay asleep in my arms.
Rest forever with my love,
till the moon will light the stars.

Calling Home

Call upon your legion,
Call it death for truth and freedom
Amid the funeral march of ghosts
We sit upon the earth that roasts
As ice shelfs fall into the ocean,
And floods infect the stinging potion.
Of a world that slept through conflict,
In mankinds selfless edict.
Where liberty drove the masses home,
To break the walls down stone by stone.

Till found was victory in the rubble,
Never fainting through it's struggle.
Through times marching killing fields,
Where liars stand to make the deals.
And subjugated was the truth,
As jubilance would burn the proof.
Where dancing fools were given nations,
High on vanities mutations.
Crying on the cloud the dead and gone,
Stolen from the earth in song.

The words of liberties true standing,
Blitzed by bombers for the compounding.
Why does the nation produce fear,
Whose flag provides for profiteer.
With wealth so deep and profits buy,
The starry banner theirs to fly.
So far away in the middle east,

That gives them all that oil to feast.
Shot downtown in warm L.A,
Who kneel not five times to pray.

The bombers gleeful in Baghdad,
Beneath the burning hated flag.
Where terror dwells to feed the beast,
Whose people fall to be deceased.
The city burns for Americas gold,
For the lies politician told.
So thousands hate and thousands die,
Please someone find out why.
Economies survive on bloodshed,
And congressman why are you not dead.

Oh what's the point don't ask me why,
The widows and the children cry
the world is spinning into doom,
We kneel and pray the holy tune.
Islam cries we are the victim,
Each bombs belated torn to sin.
Lost the reason for the conflict,
Dollar signs we hold the suspect.
Running fast are peace demanders,
Second to the war commanders.

Political manoeuvres sustain lies on CNN,
Uranium depleted shells deployed again.
Whose policy demand rational,

Thoughts of peace for international.
Lets break the power of the Imperial,
Out of touch elected remedial.
Before we lose this earth to madness,
Before the surge of Iraqs sadness.
Down below in the killing zone
They'd bomb the place you calling home.

Herbie Green

Sunshine through the rain,
Herie Green has grown again.
I smoke it through an ancient pipe,
in the haze I see the cities hype.
It doesn't matter on my cloud,
all my sanity is devoured.
I look upon this world of shit,
and toke me down another hit.
What difference does it make,
all their laws are on the take.
Don't tax my high from me tonight,
I fly into the stars so bright.
In dreamy spirals from the sky,
I float through clouds too proud and shy.
To rest upon the green blue field,
of the high to me they yield.
The bud is strong with coloured visions,
giving off these God transmissions.
Oh holy divine Herbie Green,
dance upon the vibrant scene.

Of course

Give me your heart,
before the tears start.
Down here on the streets coldness,
I need you for warmth I guess.
Did you see me crawl,
once I stood so tall.
Can you see my pride,
in me that I try to hide.
Now eternally alone,
you will not come to take me home.
My heart breaks when I hear your name,
these endless lonely nights are driving me insane.
In the rain I walk a silent hour,
my love for you is losing it's power.
Like a knife that bleeds my heart dry,
cut for the tears about you I cry.
This valley of iron where within walls you dwell,
has forgotten me and my smile does not sell.
A rose full of thorns now replaces your kiss,
and I'm asking you baby is it me that you miss.
Or am I disregarded like the pits in the strike,
bludgeoned to death by Thatchers fourth reich.
Do you remember my name,
lost in this game.
Wishing I was close to you,
can ever love be true.
I know this pain that holds me,
makes me think of liberty.
But it's just too noble to be found,

when love is sold out pound for pound.
In this world that spins for dollars,
owned and fenced by men in collars.
Do you feel the hurt,
are you alert.
Can a vision of love and unity shine for us today,
can everyone feel the same way.
Though there is no point for me and you,
because I know our love is through.
Better times are for you so nice,
and you will never see the burning fight.
Now mocking smiles from the rich empowered,
paint my banner a yellow coward.
But you cannot see that here I plead,
for rights to help me plant my seed.
Then if no rights for me will come,
then this day I meet their gun.
And in the light of sunshines warmth,
I'll sing my songs for you,
of course.

- Warrior of base -

Technicolour visionaries trapped in rooms of noise,
now for the poise.
Then it's back to base,
I saw the dragon chase.
Amid the laser beam and thump,
in the wharehouse on the dump.
The rave a swirl of masonry,
a target ot constabulary.
Colours caught the moodswing,
purple made the crowd sing.
Then charge the bill into the song,
and dance became one more wrong,
we're black and white in Babylon.
All for angel wings that lift the beat,
another letter for the sweet.
Entranced the youths until the boil,
a united beat that claimed the royal.
Then change the basic cord and code,
the party hit the open road.
Into the setting sun they blew the smoke,
around the field the word now spoke.
Liberated was the rhythms charge of free,
and all had danced in sympathy.
The swirling massive in the light,
chose the system shining bright,
walking hand in hand into the fight.
A bargain came and shouldered grief,
the price of blood condemned the thief.
Musical voids swallowed up the flare,

and trapped the trippers to it's care.
Now too hot the winding street,
though left is all the smells of sweet.
For vibrance killed the illusion,
condemning the intrusion,
when the rave fell to confusion.

White Lace

Immersed into eyes that bleed,
Your passion for another is freed.
In blessed smiles that could not touch,
My beating heart alone too much.

Where do you sleep and dream and love?
Mine is where there's stars above.
Through lonesome breaths begotten woe,
Like purest ice on winter snow.

Deliver me your flowering desire,
Lift my body from this mire.
Through broken spent emotions shell,
In tears of loneliness to dwell.

Regard this sunshine for you dear,
Bring to me your presence near.
Burn my heart each bursting beat,
Let me fly then, to defeat.

Down here I pray and so I know,
How loves devotion stays below.
But then caress igniting dreams,
Your heart belongs with fantasies.

Run out of breath collapse and cry,
Chase the dream away to fly.
Into clouds white stallions race,
To launch a rainbow through white lace.

Faithless Shame

Crocodile shop front got busted,
too many whores down south got lusted.
With truth exposed beneath a parliamentary lie,
starving Lambeth children cry.
While mum is wanted on the line,
slaving for a work tax crime.
To clean the moat and feed the dog,
Captain Kirks financial log.
Memories of trust walked away,
down a foggy lane to stay.
In the mansions of the politician,
expenses fail in recognition.
Corruption teases a blind vote,
played out for the tunes of note.
Whenever the rising cost of lies regain,
the will to walk in westminster rain.
Because hope died in the sun,
the only burning frying one.
Erect the barricades today,
fight the need to hide away.
Excuse yourself another woe,
don't miss the time and steal the show.
As the bankers wine and dine,
a billion reasons kill the crime.
When tides of deceit wash up the Thames,
a faithless shame will deny it's friends.

Spinning Free

Cascading through the drama,
is the Dalai Lama.
In a hole on the Hindu Kush,
waiting for liberation to pull and push.
Into the skies fraternity,
with the hopes of certainty.
Of wielding power from the sun,
shining like the holy one.
Constellation guiding through the seas,
balanced on twenty three degrees.
In an ocean of bitter tears,
cut up by the musketeers.
Though a lack of honour behind a Chinese wall,
defies the wind of change to call.
In Tiannamin Square the blood is spilt,
two decades of authority built.
Against a march to freedom,
waiting for a leader.
To call them out and stand them up,
to lift the masses from a damning rut.
Swapping bicycles for a four wheel drive,
the beast is here it will arrive.
To poison all the once fresh air,
that the committee can't repair.
And now the world is rusting down,
the choking score of every town.
Demand the cut of co2,
the future now depends on you.
A time has come for destiny,
to see the world that spins for free.

Siberian Zero

Stalins breath reaches into the heart,
blistered frozen torn apart.
Lifeless carcass carrion fed,
wild and fallen often bled.
A quest through pravdas ruined column,
tears soaking catastrophic foreign.
Revolution denied,
at a time ticking to decide.
The final thought against the wall,
bullet shocked too dead you fall.
Wasted passion across the steppe,
beating Trotsky on his bleeding head.
Deranged dogma paranoid hate,
Marx forgotten and unity too late.
Standing alone is one comrade hero,
freezing to death in siberian zero.

Nation Against Nation

Against turmoil sent to destroy,
Hatred and prejudice progress to deploy.
Breathing the wind again to survive,
Dreaming retribution to keep hope alive.

Decisions become a will to prepare,
All of the excuses contrived we declare.
Why liars have credence to pull you apart,
Called justification a new form of art.

Then could it be evolution of hatred divine,
Pushing their ideology to perpetrate crime.
Calling it love the desire of sacrifice,
Never again to freeze pristine polar ice.

Cauldrons of cleansing away to the fill,
Pushing the victimised to the top of the hill.
It's entertainment all these hypocrites decide,
We can make you a million if you fight for our side.

Eating the paper to satisfy greed,
All of your peasants rise to toil to be freed.
Conned by the hour a measure of sweat,
Don't cause no more problems it's all that you get.

Wealth accumulates missiles to defend the blue sky,
Have you paid for your ticket to line up and die?
I never bought reasons to burn all we eat,
And rot in the ashes of nuclear defeat.

Cold Stones

Are clouds returning to your eyes?
Like lost heartbeats in an embrace of lies.
Where you left me torn to plough desire,
In barren fields scorched dry by fire.

Dearest love decided to flee,
Into an hailstorm of precise degree.
Hurting from betrayals devious smile,
Lost wandering cold through stained beguile.

Oh counter measures stored in the heart,
Watched it all from hills where rainbows starred.
Like spies all torn to fear the change,
Lined up like victims on farces stage.

How come subterfuge clings to the past,
Making pure completion never last.
For broken skulls to bleed for kisses,
Where testimony bursts then reminisces.

I saw myself soaked in the dew,
As ghosts hurried past just walking through,
Leaving coins to satisfy a guilt trip deal,
Never touching souls with loves cheap steal.

Worn out stones unite the freed,
Surrounded by the smokes of weed.
Bought for satisfaction to cry for twice,
Un thanked for passion would not suffice.

Crossed Like The Double

You smell of streets and tear gas,
Shaking your chains like a Ho's ass
Liberty screaming in an old flow,
Guessing at freedom in a sold show.
Puking in unison on a doctors layby,
Seeing them chickens lined up for a dope pie.
Always lonely in a packed out,
Soaking up warmth as the rhymes shout.
Fading away in a world full of def jam,
Knowing too soon the blooded new lamb.
Wherever we go it's full like a moonbeam,
A future decided to blow like a coal seam.
Clashing in fields for a new lease,
Echoing the shout from graves of a decease.
Yea man fuck da police.
Nothing ain't neat.
Listen in sucker to the call of a new beat,
Bouncing off walls in a nation of obese.
Slim it down muther,
Don't attack the dreams of another.
You know it's so easy to judge a new hit,
Calling for honeys with the hope of a warm tit.
Smokin all over the realm of an old foe,
Stealing the blow in a world of no go.
Can't you see me there holding back the tears of struggle,
It ain't me out there brother being crossed like the double.

The Light of Russias Torch

The crowning moment of evenings song that by which are forged within our dreams to light the darkened hours of dooms devices.

Another breathless retreat might well destroy any consolidation that the bravest would dig deep to muster even into deaths quaint endings.

It is our dream before another round of huddled moments at the

fires of our encampments with blazing eyes in vodkas courage we do dance.

Our rising expectations in the very last corner of each faint gasp and cry of torment till each will win the prize of suicides carefree jaunt.

As thrown into the winds of undesireable odds we have sent our best to rally without glory but for the gutbusting terror of our fury.

Regret not your fallen comrades dying embrace and tears of spent emotion in the face of evil taunts to surrender.

Before it was our armistice we carried in our banners that meant

little,

we drank away our fear with vodkas smiling winged flurry. And in the freezing suns of evening times biting winds each shot we swig igniting new dreams of each martyred som of a whore.

We were damned before each battl cry,
we were damned from the pulpit,
in villages and towns,
hated and despised,
feared and beguiled.

But in the zeal of headstrong passions we rose to counter act
barbarianism to destroy the envious gossip that our cause would
fall asunder.
It was with bitter tears I knew realities convulsions as lakes
of blood tossed waves in the storms of each rising.

The dream we held,
the golden sickle.

Our hearts united in songs of great rejoicement marching arm
in arm toward the tiger rising as a monster against my
motherland
Many wept and ran weaponless into certain deaths fixed price
falling like trees before the axemans gleeful tally.
Till we saw the dawn of exhaustion creep to destroy the
monsters
disregard,
and we thawed our disrespect into boiling cauldrons of our
contempt. Till like the fire itself we swept and leapt on the
rising winds of devine consultation. Till we convinced Nike
herself that she owed her allegiance to our motherland our
Soviet
our Russia.

The World that came in Third

Acid death,
at 100mph.
Off the cliffs of time,
into eternities smiling crime.
Cursed through blood,
the touching dud.
Over times long road,
to the gates of Hades load.
Where normal odes ceace to tame,
when everything just looks the same.
Passing fields where crops are grown,
in the summertime love is sown.
But into my heart of stone tonight,
only my star is burning bright.
Because all smiles will cease to burn,
for they forbid the truth to learn.
To buy the deal and snort it fast,
you come up too soon when fear is last.
When casualties die down on the ward,
bleeding before the rays of dawn.
That touch your face and burn your tears,
when nations turn away from ears.
Because agenda taught me lies,
everyday the media tries.
To deflect the truth from being seen,
when all the stories are obscene.
So nevermind the burning sun,
we never bought the last oil drum.

They burnt it for the lie they sell,
the flames they flourish in Baghdad's hell.
Though we never thought we could be heard,
in the world that came in third.

Sarejevo 2

Was this heart entwined too long in your desire,
though we did nothing to presume forgiveness.
Returning from even heavier futility,
we left love with doubts and never to guess.
All our city was a disregarded site,
with all our worth left crying in tatters.
Your eyes though pierced the muddy retreats,
where we saved all that ever matters.
Lost in a longing smile,
too heavy the sky to hold my tears.
On my hopes your heart has rested,
where never the sun has shone for years.

Sarejevo, Sarejevo,
the dead corpse of a lover.

Sarejevo, Sarejevo,
never again will I hold her.

Sarejevo, Sarejevo,
the ripped guts of a city.

Sarejevo, Sarejevo,
love, peace and unity.

Artistic Crime

Between these blessed hearts we have chosen our delight,
in this glorious warmth can I beckon to you for no delay
to bring in this lively night.
For in this evenings fadeing glow we will see with new eyes
our true belief,
defined in reasons why we stole there will be our happy thief.

What we have sought has been gathered in like treasure,
secrecy now reigns between us and we speak of things with
measure.
Hidden beneath the bustle of this wooded glade,
are prizes gathered that we accumulate and raid.
Unseen in the bustling city we slip hitherto without anyones
perception,
each intention we covet in hearty silence as we sup the ales
of crimes correction.

Some have mentioned sorrow,
some have slipped away to kneel at the forgiving gaze of angels
statues.
Though dedication, till we have counted our fortune is what
beholds within our circle of content,
The contention of a mutual honour,
till one or all have faced detection,
into captivity charged and sentenced.

Justice

State that ideas come neatly to pay,
Gross overpricing so richman can play.
With the lives of his minions in every war,
Controlling the markets to oppress the poor.

Why is it always morally right,
To open the banks up to hoard cash to fight.
When blood in the gutters spills for a beer,
With widows now suffering pouring the tear.

Has leadership become a move into conflict,
Settling disputes to solve like a con trick.
On the T.V liars try to justify hate,
With rallied up children thinking it's great.

Tensions on borders waiting there still,
All the excuses progress to the kill.
Political manoeuvres collect up desire,
To match codes for the missiles ready to fire.

Hey peacemaker where are you can you find some pride,
Is it terror inside you making you hide.
Voice your opinion if you still have one left,
Don't leave without saying your countries bereft.

Has love become prejudice to ease in the score,
Racist governors in papers proclaiming for more.
Hanging the truth up to justify lies,
Was it always this way sir this corpse then replies.

Solstice

Surfing mornings beating drum,
I dance beneath a solstice sun.
As mists of dawn run to a quiet earth,
I witness days of golden worth.

Where pounds are precious on the street,
strumming odes where spirits meet.
Again we steal a dying crime,
to coin each phrase we feel sublime.

Clouds are sleepy around sunrays,
in blazing artistry it always pays.
The measure due to hit this land,
where poets bleed just where they stand.

Waking glory asks for more,
on street corners true to score.
Intensity brews a passing glance,
to nurture seeds of first romance.

Pilgrims post was left deserted,
in long hours when love came flirting.
Settling kisses sweet like candy,
in a ghostly moonbeams dark calamity.

Calling earths desire to touch,
each young angel loved up much.
To kiss another breeze this time,
around sunshines blazing mime.

Whenever we rejoice and sing,
for future hope that love may bring.
In forgiving waves of loves device,
we breathe the freshest wind of ice.

Yet candles lit tell stories too,
ablaze to burn the word in you.
In heartbeats unburdened 'neath the sky,
for in dawns battalion you will not cry.

Caustic

I can feel it in me,
tormented rotations vibing again.
Reaching into a heart withdrawn,
seeking lust from only pain.

Your eyes hurt beyond measure,
never feeling romances death.
Touching voids of notoriety,
blazing words till each last breath.

Down around midnights spell,
where tears rejoice untimely ghosts.
Working liberties burnt anger,
sacrificing hearts to roast.

Beyond powers tripping needs,
another chance burns loves demise.
Beckoning home desires flirtation,
bedded on these fraternal lies.

Then never holding onto sunshine,
needing avenues to wander.
Leaving dusk in nightmarish issue,
alone to weep and sit and ponder.

Free me then this hurt's so absolute,
denying all that soothing logic.
Tasting blood from empty moonbeams,
feeling lost insane so caustic.

Make The Deal

Sky is ablaze on eastern borders,
butchers thieves are under orders.
Hope decides to hide till midnight,
when your stars detail the fight.
Behind a lovelorn body of lies,
in the gutters of broken pride.
Where another myth may drink us under,
denying the rage of man made thunder.
On bomblasts cue we cry again,
inflicted with this nurtured pain.
Then reality will find the score unreal,
in rhythms of a tune we steal.
Bloody deals will cry out for you,
to rejoin the fight with glue.
Behind the lie that grows then flinches,
defeating death by only inches.
Back at base we sigh and wonder,
at the bombers works that plunder.
When blitzed again a heart explodes,
from this hate that nothing holds.
Due to reasons that the thieves may bleed,
we'll kick the prisoners that we freed.
For the evidence was crass,
and through the fighting we attack.
To release bullets into bodies broken,
to fund each death with party tokens.
Down beside a common touch,
when all the dying gets too much
Whilst polocies can only steal,
the criminals will cut a deal.

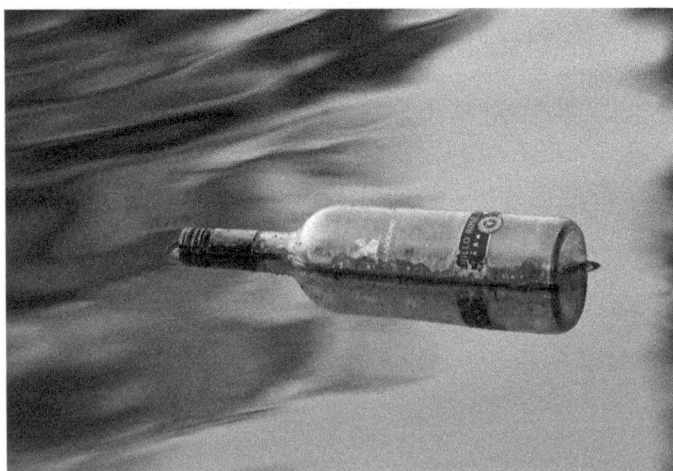

Eternal Wine

Oh fade now sun your day has passed,
that orange, purple slide has crashed.
Greet the darkness come devour,
daylights hold on burning power.
For that star my heart is bought,
to my love for kisses taught.
Blue velvet sky has come to cover,
all my heart to dream a lover.
Were you not here oh blessed one,
to kiss my passionate heart, a drum.
I hold you near to liberate,
my cracking bones from futile hate.
Before the mountains gained their height,
your heart was near throughout the night.
And pleasant winds caressed my soul,
then formed me to a person whole.
I see your face inside my head,
I see your eyes the tears they've bled.
One touch will heal your broken will,
to lay beside me quiet and still.
Like the night you are a mystery,
to free me from the darkest misery.
Then run through fields of amber corn,
where a path to love is worn.
Take me to the forest drove,
bed me down with all I own.
Lose not the light the moon will shine,
and taste me your eternal wine.

Retro

Waking up tomorrow,
snow storm seemed to last for fifteen days.
Thinking about your karma,
leading spiral stairs to trip my brains.
Your colours all precede me,
shining rainbow paths beneath my feet,
logic lost to reason.
Music comes alive to your heartbeat.
Slowly, truly my eyes are open wide to your sure move,
don't think just touch lips that shine a quest for
love to prove.

Revolution Walk

Bullets choke indoctrination,
blazing realisms blank citation.
In courtrooms of ideals presuming,
freedoms needs when deaths are looming.

Amongst a massive in decline,
threatening to forge a crime.
Before laws of mundane optimism,
protects the assets of capitalism.

Inside the doctrine of the poor,
where deaths decline to oppress more.
Because to liberate communes dwelling,
life belies beneath states now falling.

Renewed terror holds the key,
to release again our seduction free.
Though arbitration falls when bullets strike,
to destroy ages brand new Reich.

Across a seething hatred sore,
bursting in a myth they explore.
To continue struggle through closed eyes,
that expropriates the hearts of all mankind.

Where does action meet the meek,
battered on demonstration street.
Daring to stand up the talk,
and walk the revolution walk.

Desert Bloom

Tripping the wires of communication,
a desert floor comes into bloom.
I saw flowers grow in rain and sunshine,
and picked a few to scent my room.

Pink sky fills all,
the sun slows purple to a crawl.
As night engulfs the day,
each time it is this way.
waiting for another rise,
walking to the ocean through a desert full of
lonely cries.

Sky of cold dark night,
sending shivers through the rocks.
Appearance like a statue,
taking up at least ten blocks.
We find shelter from the icy breeze,
then she begins to kiss and tease,
until the sun gets off it's knees.

Bright explosion of another dawn,
the blazing sky a crown of thorns.
To the ocean I set my sight,
we get there before last daylight.

See the drowning sun hiss across the skies,
the colours blend a glory now reflected in my eyes.
Beach and water in rhythm like a slow dance,
sends the yearning for submersion into a summer trance.

Blaze the Sun

Was the day too far to see,
through the clouds of misty free.
In the CS gas device,
around the summit warm and nice.
Where sat the guilded ties,
with their polocies and lies.
That cost the earth it's dignity,
to the tune of sanity.
Grave now the position of the riot,
to demonstrate anger and not deny it.
Across the global spectrum,
stand off and don't elect them.
One day at the barricades we'll sing,
for the fight that each will bring.
To bear the truth of freedoms blood,
from a trickle to a flood.
With broken skulls that crack to say,
defend the poor so that we may.
Unite for international respect,
to democratically elect.
The representation of our cause,
to fight the history of wars.
That divide us for their wealth and hate,
to starve us at the richmans gate.
Where hopelessness says that we,
are defeated without unity.
Call the banners out today,
let them glory the sunray.
The masters shake each time we fight,

so scared of our unbroken might.
From histories defiance to,
accept their laws that oppress you.
Then martyred inside the ideal,
you live forever with what we feel.
As clouds roll past to nobodies drum,
the sky is free to blaze the sun.

Anna Kournikova

Anna Kournikova,
advantage to as angelic muscles tense.
The crowd holds breaths,
a ray of sun shines through golden hair.
I forget the score and all the care.
If she wins another day we'll see,
Anna Kournikova a champion be.

Strawberries and cream,
rain and sunshine inside the dream.
Centre court womens final day,
oh win Anna Kournikova I pray.
Tomorrow it will be,
colour photo's in the press for me.

She'd just love my dream,
a Russian ace goes by unseen.
And then Anna Kournikova is the Wimbledon champ,
and me, well I'll always be a tramp.
Though one with more photo's of,
Anna Kournikova.

Touch me

Touch me sunshine,
listen to my heart cry.
Dance in circles cool breeze,
lift my spirit to fly.

Crawled from the gutter I did,
in rags that told the nightmare.
The wind whispered softly,
she told me who would care.

Still the smiling sun,
caught the light of noon.
Said tomorrow took a day,
and not an hour too soon.

There is no doubting love,
on the cracked pavement where I sat.
Watching people come along,
to put money in my hat.

Then I eat fresh food,
and drink down summer wines.
I think of the loves I lost,
past now happy times.

See the ocean calling me,
old friend of ancient power.
Place the sea shells on your eyes,
and she will be your lover.

I know in dreams of truth,
each day begins new breath.
I caste my tears to the floor,
for each yesterdays a death.

Can you spare the time dear sun,
to bring me clear the vision.
Of a land that blossoms love,
where healing is your mission.

Touch me sunshine,
touch me ocean clear.
Wash me into wonderful,
wipe away this tear.

Blood of Innocence

See the judge ruling you,
feel the pain cutting through.
Your sentence comes as no surprise,
banged to rights by a torrent of lies.
In the time it took to say,
your life in pleads away.
They rolled you neatly for the price,
and toasted victory on ice.
Now outside the walled confusion,
their free within a new delusion.
High on pills and dopes new vanity,
singing songs just for insanity.
Lost in perceptions of deceit,
blind to marching jackboot feet.
Across the land the mist comes down,
people say that life is a clown.
Nothings real until death,
counts the cost of each last breath.
Crawling on it's knees is liberty,
searching for a lost fraternity.
To find the damned of the division,
to fulfill the aims of a futile mission.
Though all at sea you are with the captain,
through a storm that you are trapped in.
The winds a demon to the fool,
and freedoms a pigeon on a stool.
You cannot forget the treachery,
it burns inside legality.

To break the chains of who you are,
to unleash the vision and the star.
It burns inside your brain for real,
that you are a slave to every meal.
In ashes you will sit and cry,
and shake your fists to why oh why.
Answers come after the bullet,
as you cash in hate for a bloody wallet.
When it's all gone in darkest time,
you'll have revenge that once was mine.

Seasons come

Feeling down,
lost the reason for this frown.
Got up this morning feeling wild,
could it be I'm the only child.
But calling quietly was summer,
causing me to rise from slumber,
in the glorious wonder.
Where seagulls fly dreams unite,
passions visit me at night.
Though reality leaves me cold,
as the seasons grow me old.
The wind does float my heart to you though,
keep me warm through winter snow.
Oh to be within your arms,
with no cares like winters charms.
In spring bring me cool fresh water,
to touch my lips reviving splendour.
Bring to me sweet cup victorious,
that it may rejuvenate and glory us.
Forging peace where once was bitterness,
leave for battle but come back to love,
let peace be for the earth a glove.
Oh why is the world so bare,
of the likes of those who care.
Where bullets smile on dead faces,
shot from the guns of all the races.
It leaves me shivering in the sun,
it leaves me crying like a son.

Lost in hatred times evolving,
cut to pieces the worlds revolving.
In these days of melting polar ice,
and the weathers not so nice.
But who does care for warring nature,
man is blind to his own stature.
As heavy oceans spit pollution,
onto the cliffs of it's confusion.
Where reason are you,
where sanity is true.
Come alive new rainbow soldier,
rise to be the earths new saviour.
Bring the bows of peace to conquer,
kiss the earth to show we love her.
Revive the splendour we have left,
heal the crazy who of peace are bereft.
Has the times destruction come,
and if so where have we to run.

Stop

Stop killing our earth,
for profit is your only worth.
Sky was blue and ocean clear,
now clouded by mans profit dear.

Rape of nature carries ever on,
warrior of rainbow hear my song.
Take arms of courage from the pure,
and fight pollution with love as cure.

The Rhythm

The very first pulse,
coming through the darkness in my mind.
Till then awake to the sound I find.
I find melody,
rhythm of tranquility.
All hazy flowers,
psychedelic hours.
Continuation through the soul,
exact percussion is the goal.

Gospel choir invites the vibe,
as rhythm and blues is flying the tribe.
Addictive beats recoil on air,
as we dance through the mist without a care.
Energy brings new pulsation,
we call the radio station.
All is hippy shake,
and we are ready for another take.

The music of a hidden meadow,
in the boating jackets of an English ghetto.
Amid the sunrays of an evening,
with the lyrics that you have to sing.
We are lazy in our need to fly,
like the smiling ghosts of a paisley tie.
In the swelter of a summers day,
we love the rhythm here to stay.

Cliffs of Dover

You are so lovely like flowers in the sun,
like daydreaming of your embrace and kisses.
Oh like nothings real except you.
All the others fade away,
I feel so lonely in this world of blue.
Touch me make me shiver,
make me warm so cold I am.
Bless your eyes and your heart,
I worship this feeling,
I know I am dreaming.
Could you ever be mine?.
Hurting bad my heart beats painfully,
when you are close I feel such a fool,
to have this emotion for you.
Poets dream away on clouds,
poets cry of love unfound.
These yearning words need your kiss,
how can all life come to this.
In times of lonely minutes past,
to hours without you sweetest love.
But your hearts for another,
with kisses for your lucky lover.
I'm sorry everything feels empty,
I'm poor and lost tattered and free.
This love I have is flying over,
my English Rose,
the cliffs of Dover.

Flowers of the Field

Where tears have fallen poppies sing,
a tune of healing the wind does bring.
Beneath the blue sky now is peace,
an aching calm brings war to ceace.
Fields of France lost love lies under,
the blood soiled earth asleep till thunder.
Wakes the sleeping souls at rest,
where now my love I sleep the best.
An age gone by all but forgotten,
a generation lost long now all rotten.
The red flower sold to a sunrays dream,
now birds at play in a world serene.
Never forget the peace white dove,
abide not in fear but live for love.
The world moves on but still we die,
still we mourn and still we cry.
In fields of silence white crosses stand,
laid together in a foreign land.
When we are all gone who will care,
for the bravery that put them there.
Shout aloud to gain Gods ear,
ask him to destroy all fear.
Though nations still prepare for battle,
humanity the butchered cattle.
Is this then in my hand a rose?,
for world peace is what I've chose.
Don't laugh and say more war will come,
blinded by the midday sun.

Silence of the Hush

Walking down the darkened road,
like innocence for the untold.
Where gathers evil in the midst,
of wealth and treachery well spent.
Without the guide of martyred life,
in the morn' of the last light.
Before the shadows fell to govern,
the temperature in a global oven.
First fell freedom by the sword,
then fell truth for we were bored.
Away ran liberty to find the sane,
to tell our history who to blame.
Wake the waves to bloat and wreck,
the polar ice will split the deck.
Now minions elected lie,
to bake the cake of Gucci pie.
From mountain ranges pity weeps,
for nothings hers and nothing keeps.
Blasting bombs evoke slept satan,
who drinks the blood of every nation.
Selling souls the fat cat smiles,
his polocy of hate beguiles.
Where nothing grows except our tears,
a sacrifice learnt well for years.
The end must come so we begin,
to weigh the cost of suffering.
Before the might of natural doom,
drowns us in the great monsoon.

What is left to count as pure,
in a spinning world without a cure.
Where's the switch to pour the light,
on dignities begotten fight.
Where next the bomber drops the load,
into the cities that explode.
Like carnivals of evil taunts,
the victor gets all that he wants.
The spoil of war is golden black,
pouring from wounded Iraq.
Into the mouth and it's well guzzled,
because Uncle Sam was never muzzled.
The merchants of the statistic loss revived,
a dying boy with all their lies.
And left with heads crowned with gold,
a champion we now behold.
Can you see the fuming cloud?,
mushrooming to engulf the crowd.
Wake with fear but don't deny,
the words of peace that now we cry.
Whose satisfaction rules for fear?,
who pays the cheque?, the profiteer.
And down the drain our labour pours,
in the festering wound of the earths sores.
Bring the touch that heals tonight,
denounce the richness of their might.
Suicidal dreams are for the pure,
who search the world to find a cure.

Surrender nothing slash and burn,
when you see the corner turn.
Don't look back to smile at Bush,
hear the silence of the hush.
Before the roar of mighty men,
who come to save us all again.

Cambridge Square

All the places I have been,
haunt me now in every dream.
I was alone in stormy days,
searching for some golden rays.

You left me in a dark cold void,
empty lost and paranoid.
The compass in my brain was broken,
every word for lies was spoken.

You never loved me now I know,
this victim of your cruel show.
Now I'm strong and I don't care,
how you left me in that Cambridge square.

Don't say you love me now my dear,
oh how you love to lie and sneer.
For it's all over and lost in time,
and now my heart is only mine.

Ghetto Chase

Beneath the midday sun,
I saw you run.
Into the arms,
that held for you no charms.
For fear has become real,
and I know how you must feel.
But it really doesn't matter,
because we've heard the latest chatter.
Down here on the street,
we're always standing neat.
Ready all the while,
to wear the latest style.
But yours is going out,
a wiseman saw your doubt.
And now your running scared,
in the heat that we prepared.
It's a long way to the cover,
of another doting lover.
When you are worn by ageing tears,
that flood to drown your fears.
In the ghetto of the lost,
everything will cost.
The price is soaring high,
into the blazing sky.
And it's something you can't meet,
when you've nothing left to eat.
So the penny jar is broken,
for the needs you left unspoken.

In reality it's hard vice,
snorting what was nice.
Thats left you chasing visions,
of a messiahs quiet transmissions.
Of a gleaming rulers throne,
thats taken all you own.
In the ghetto lights go out,
because they know what you are about.
And they've left you all alone,
looking for a home.
Far away over hills,
the hunter makes his kills.
He owns a race for profit,
but the truth is love don't want it.

Erupt the Sun

Reach into sunbeams through the cloud,
Attempt to smile if rain pours down.
Touch your breath to stir a breeze,
Stand to call through summers tease.

Saw you once beneath the low,
Wondered about your loveless glow.
In times resourceful beckoned touch,
Amid the tulips of the Dutch.

Dancing butterfly come near,
Rackets sell your souvenir.
To pay a price that love beheld,
The ransom of your newly shelved.

Shake off your fears of colours flown,
Beside the rivers flowing home.
Nutrition buys a drink to sell,
Your thirst to fight and then to tell.

Notorious delivered and declined,
The contract we agreed and signed.
Rising in this covenant,
The colours of our rainbow chant.

I never knew your smile could kill,
I waited long and then until.
We saw the dawn erupt the sun,
And how it shone to then become.

September Sun

That first tender kiss I am sure you recall,
left me in chains that led me to fall.
Turn around and show me your smile,
it was not for love that you lived in denial.

Come a long way since the autumn of tears,
come a long way since a call to deaf ears.
Why is it this reason was the ultimate end?,
when I'm losing a lover not gaining a friend.

I remember the endless fields of poppy flowers,
stretching for miles that we walked through for hours.
It's remarkable now that we could not evade,
our kisses for passion without getting laid.

Call me anytime I come with the sun,
make me a tune and my life for a drum.
Pour me another that seems to bring smiles,
or is it the hour that puts our kiss into files?.

Loving you was never easy,
leaving you was never come.
So why my dear are you crying?,
beneath this warm September sun.

I just cannot help the time that passes,
each day we lose means missing chances.
The colour of your eyes enhances all we cried for to be true,
another line say's I'm hurting inside,
for the outside misses you.

Inglorious Crime

Finding the shade to cool from the sun,
I walk into the ever blaze of today.
My eyes are playing tricks with the reflection I caste,
in the shop window my smile flew away.

But it's allright for I've never lost with my gun,
and it's too soon to say or to tell her she's won.
Do you think I am an interest that will rise in percent,
will I profit a smile from her lips scent?.

My babies far away from the vale,
the euphoria I bought to remind me was ale.
And I found time to regret every touch,
that has captured my heart and I am loving too much.

And I don't know how long I've been walking,
now all my colours have bled from suppourting.
Should I never feel her again close at night,
when we're lost in the rhythm and she holds me tight.

I think I saw the bridge where we sighed,
for the willow is near the place where you cried.
Aloud with my name you fell into my arms,
and admitted defeat in the hail of my charms.

Before we sleep tonight they will prepare for the dawn,
a beautiful chorus the birds bring in the morn'.
However we feel before this sunrise display,
will never lay seige to our love on it's way.

Simply the reason for this mutual respect,
for there is never a lie that is easy to detect.
Although in the truth we can wallow again,
and ignore all the fear and the heartache and pain.

Comfort me then for I have seen a lost nation,
inside my mind I am far from elation.
As we count on each breeze for the air's being bought,
as we blindly walk on with this faith we are taught.

Come and sit around my fire and talk of tomorrow,
is it love you are fighting behind the wall of your sorrow.
So cry if your wish was forgotten in time,
spend your tears on my love for the inglorious crime.

Wisdom Now Compete

Along a road of stricken tears,
In relentless sunshine for these years.
For times reduction shelling fields,
To break the fountain of your deals.

Pouring from veins of gold,
Are profits for the lies we left untold.
Regardless fools can beg for bread.
And swill it down till truth is dead.

Wandering across a blue torn sky,
Clouds of reluctance can now apply.
For a vacant smile that can now forgive,
As long as children sing to live.

Dodge a hailstorm of bursting shells,
Destroy the production of oil wells.
Search for policies of deceit,
Till all your leaders face defeat.

Wise amid constructed lies,
Concoct a story for media cries.
Give them blood that they deserve,
To liberate fight and to observe.

It's not too long till roads of blood,
Or tears of widows shed to flood.
Decide then to become our peace,
And seek your wisdom now complete.

Situations vacant, I

Situations vacant, I,
look toward timeless quarter pie.
Delinquence of attitude,
blank during the interlude.
Naked eyes amongst the smoke,
pass along the final toke.
Time to wake from hazy days,
summer come through springtime praise.
Greens and blues and sunshine colours,
wash through soaring kestral feathers.
And rhyme leads onto oceans,
natures locomotions.

Stretch the soul to yawn aloud,
then fly through cotton wool type cloud.
Bathe in sunrays that caress not burn,
sing of joys you quest to learn.
Take along no apprehensions,
and find your true contentions.
Breeze the winds that trade the pollen,
Cross the river that now has swollen.
For love now flows free,
with natures first degree.

Song To Fight

Song flooded hearts entwined,
Liberating lovers blind.
Bargaining for a touch desired,
Into eyes of burning fires.

Serenade the bullets flowing,
Through the night the killers knowing.
Destined in a vacant smile,
To blow the task of loves denial.

Rhyming Californian scum,
Naked bleeding on the run.
Thinking rays of sun declare,
Fashions crime of debonair.

Fluctuate these market dollars,
Wired and booted to the collars.
Plundered coastlines crumble down,
Remarkable comments coastal town.

Besiege the mind with L.S.D,
Say the lie that you are free.
Count your blessings to the till,
Sell your country for the thrill.

Anthems rally up the cry,
Death and glory oh to die.
MP say this time we're right,
Liberty and freedom means we fight.

L'arc Enciel

Apparitions blown through smiles,
Cheerful rendition into scenes beguiles.
Inside a myths continued dream,
Thinking raindrops fall pristine.

Becalmed a voice that strained to tell,
Stories broken onto rocks that fell.
Through chasms believed to be divine,
Into streets with bloods defaulted crime.

Where do you breathe away and cry,
Into clouds L'arc enciel will sigh.
To carry wealth away and steal,
Leaving broken teeth to fail and deal.

Aware confronted and denied,
Pouring oceans where all have cried.
Because the score was sold to bare,
The gnashing teeth of who knows where.

Meadows in an English sun,
Rare and beautiful to stun.
A glimpse of paradise to dwell,
Drained emotions stolen shell.

Can't dream tonight a moon may say,
Clouds have drifted me away.
I shine at commands of winds device,
Onto the oceans scene now thrice.

Oceans Swell

A sky so vast to wander lost,
Or search for in your beauties cost.
A price so long to hold with fire,
Burning like the suns desire.

Flying ever to the eastern star,
On winds that beckon home your heart.
Flourishing in your pure warm breeze,
To bring my passion to it's knees.

Call my eyes a black wondrous fate,
Use your strengths to designate.
Where opinions gather to decide,
Where liars run away to hide.

Oh I know truth has become real.
From my treasures liars steal.
To hoard deceits throne of greed,
And say through teeth that you are freed.

In light I walk into the sun,
Pleasant wind destroys the gun.
And damning empires crumble down,
Brick by brick and town by town.

Are we near yet dearest one?
My eyes are tired and sleep must come.
Touch my heart for dreams may tell,
Of storms across an oceans swell.

Sarejevo 1

These shattered walls of lost innocence,
down the alleyways of stark reality.
We can see the damages of doctrine,
the tearful march of new columns of refugee.
And nothing will ever change,
and no man will help stem the blood.
For there is not bravery here today,
only womens tears flowing to a flood.
They mourn not only loved and lost ones,
but also their country now a leper.
There is no investment for their cities,
no one comes near to wager.

Sarejevo, Sarejevo,
the bullet marked walls.

Sarejevo, Sarejevo,
the mortars blown your balls.

Sarejevo, Sarejevo,
we call on you to bring peace.

Sarejevo, Sarejevo,
stop the war and ceace.

Seventh Sea

Call aboard your misery,
that we might greet the seventh sea.
And glide by ages past now gone,
to sing to me the eleventh song.
Bring the clouds that soak you cold,
I will give my hand to hold.
Between the darkest howls of night,
my smile will be your sunshine bright.
Passing the island of the dead,
we drink the wine we poured so red.
And dream of eternal winds to push,
the tide up to the Hindu Kush.
Drowning follies cry for help,
keep hold of the saving rope.
That we may save ourselves from you,
who were not just and pure and true.
Again the thrash of awesome gales,
whip us to speed and kiss our sails.
To heights ungained where mortals ceace,
to grasp the truth and bring no peace.
The storm buys electric and fantasia,
we drink the wine that freed our rage here.
And cruising to the birth of time,
we shake our bones to beat the crime.
Falling free into the sea,
was liberties grown dignity.
Then to the depths we sunk our frowns,
to never sell our souls for pounds.

Asleep now wind when once a roar,
you said the rich stole from the poor.
And rest was given between toil,
the ship sailed on the storm to foil.

Obscene

Downstairs is a dismal,
rat infested woe.
I'm out here in the darkness,
waiting for the show.

Call me over anxious,
it's raining in my soul.
Pay me what my dues are,
I'm scoring for the dole.

In disasters reigning magic,
down here near the spikes.
I'm dreaming of old china,
cruising along on bikes.

Never seeing sunshine,
in wilderness's dream.
My thoughts are blown to pieces,
my words are all obscene.

Loves Embrace

The sea dazzled like ten million diamonds,
in the swelter of eternal suns.
If I could possess just one that shines,
more sought than from South African mines.
I would place it on your cheek and dream,
in your arms for longer than eternity.
Mere words could not convince your heart,
no kisses could begin to start.
The beating of my own will race,
at the beauty of your lovely face.
That glows in summers radiant life,
to bathe in the glorious light.
Soothing away the pain I feel,
when you go away my heart you steal.
In times of cloudless skies I faint,
into the sea that made us great.
Say my name and touch me deep,
all my life is yours to keep.
Though ignorance may call me naive,
I live for you so please believe.
Oh summer sun awake for glory,
it's life a lovers untold story.
But now I sleep inside your soul,
each breath you take can make me whole.
Where once was emptiness now filled,
now is life that once was killed.
Alive the sky so empty and warm,
defying summers need to storm.
Like racing waves we rise and fall,
in loves embrace we stand so tall.

Rock 'n' Rolling

Devastating dreams tumble through my mind,
calling for the light to shine upon mankind.
In darkness gripped with tears,
panic grows within the sneers.
Where love became a joke,
laughed at in the poke.
Forever wasted through tomorrow,
in a world we only borrow.
Whenever heartbeats miss each time,
in the dustbins near the crime.
Because laughter bought a dud,
infiltrating through your blood.
That was spilt among the wrongs,
when the dead sang all the songs.
Through a river bodies float,
whilst all the ministers lie and gloat.
For cuts dismantle all the good,
like the deals down in the hood.
Where humanity haemorrhages truth,
down dignities dying route.
In a road plan for some peace,
in a war of wealth to fleece.
Throughout times devices,
knocking doors to heal with spices.
In a trade becoming lost and stolen,
profits falling tough not golden.
And again troops fly off home,
after Mad Max in the Thunderdome.
Because the deals been rigged beholding,
as all the troops were rock 'n' rolling.

Famine

I walked a long long lonely mile,
without any,
yes without some.
In my mind a cry was heard,
then I see fields of red stretched for miles, I.
I stutter with new expression,
hungry on my knees,
asking for love from a light sweeping breeze.
They never listen,
the world is deaf.
This course has hardened dryness,
the sky harsh and burning.
A sun so great I fear.
My bones enlarge on shrinking skin,
it can become my death here.
I fade in hopelessness,
where is release from pain.

Distant Shore

Pour upon this distant shore,
The word of lifes eternal poor.
When rainclouds gather around the sun,
Call upon your spirit guide to come.

For overland we marched for truth,
To convey the words of freedoms proof.
Where tears had nurtured trees so strong,
To make us all on earth belong.

The love I lost was rare and true,
Amid the gunfire blasting through.
As peace prevailed not long,
Snuffed out like a dead mans song.

Across fields for shelter we persist,
There to clench a hand into a fist.
And forge together our strength to fight,
For loves renewed preparation light.

The pipers fall to silence they,
Down on their knees a strength to pray.
But like the ballistic bombs that blast,
Explosions tear like missiles fast.

In time we rise to greet our dawn,
To bathe in blood we shed to warn.
And cry our tears till middays sun,
Has raced the day till moons become.

The Reader

When innocent begot profound,
Through a tangled nuance of wrecked morality.
Which colour brought forth renewed attire?
In the realm of an epoch of insanity.

Down rail tracks of designed industry,
Mass feeding of an evil foe.
Historic notions of repressed prejudice,
Equalled only by barbaric woe.

The edges untied with logic,
No reasoning pounces from the page.
As society still reals with horror,
As countries clash with wars and rage.

Injustice meets the unjust juror,
No future beckons all they lost.
By the hands of mad men's dogma,
Fleeing from the verdicts cost.

Where blame can never find the culprit,
An illiterate massive grows and dies.
And evidence was blown impassive,
Amid the horror of six million cries.

Madmen drank the deep repression,
Fuelled and driven on by hatreds vine.
And victims rose to reap some justice,
Though lost in truth the guilt's no crime.

Sunshine Days

This time I see the sun,
rising above the fields to freedom, run.
The day is racing toward my eyes,
your smile cuts me down to size.
I stand in the empty air,
searching for something that is not there.
A smiling butterfly knows the way,
knows there is something more to say.
Flowers glory in the sunshine bright,
woken up from sleepy night.
I stretch my arms and feeling alive,
I love to dance the living jive.
Come this way all world and see,
the radiant sun that shines so free.
Distant clouds shy away,
chirping birds are busy at pray.
It is alive this land so rare,
wooded glades that need not care.
The rolling hills of Englands grace,
never the chains of slavery to face.
It feels so good to shout aloud,
the words we love that make us proud.
Give me your smile oh free white dove,
touch the breeze that feathers love.
Call my name and beautify,
all the things that make us cry.
Dry your tears in summer rays,
and hope for never ending sunshine days.

Song

Are the fires inside,
just along for the ride.
Down the gleaming road of memory,
to the corner of insanity.
Where I lost you there forever,
in a world of lies and never.
For the view into my heart,
was frozen from the start.
And your tears of ice could hurt,
when love was not the word.
Then if we had never met,
no kisses of regret.
Could ever hold me down,
in this lonely town.
Where the best have since left,
the cold streets now of life bereft.
Beneath clouds crazy patterns,
only sunshine ever matters.
For we dream diamonds and gold,
as we grow to become old.
In a world we only rent,
till we are doubled up and bent.
For the weight of all the tears,
drown you through the years.
When you saw your vision,
in secrecy a mission.
Like a ghost you walked away,
in silence through the day.

Now the darkness of the night,
is all that holds me tight.
And the memories have gone,
since I drowned myself in song.

Death on Tour

Are you now sure that life could yield,
Resurrection amid hopes torn battlefield.
Of clashed ideals that broke factions away,
From pursuing the peace that your leaders betray.

Dancing through the poppy strewn meadow,
Corpses applaud the cleansed empty ghetto.
Down steel rails of bleeding dumb smiles,
Ghosts epitomise the reminder of your mocking show trials.

Ancient gatherings hold onto plain wisdom,
A knowledge lost woefully to modern Christendom.
For prophecies culminate in worn out prejudice,
Reprised in doctrines that equate the abyss

Hunted down for someone's entertainment,
News at ten decide issues to implement.
Desires to foul to rejoice and indoctrinate,
For salaries impotent for labours of pure hate.

Why does it rain upon your pageantry,
To exclude the enemies of your majesty?
Who sits with liars to create legislation,
That's passed to corrupt your deals with temptation.

It's legal punishment to create deceit,
On the front pages the liars full up to complete.
In mansions they've decided to show you the door,
My wander through reason proclaimed death on tour.

In Retrospect

Talking revolution in the dark,
Between the bus stop and the park.
Smoke some fags and plot to kill,
The government and the old bill.

Sleep with dreams of Thatcher on the block,
Oh yes her head is for the chop.
Wake up sweating feeling scared,
Of all the hate that she prepared.

Miners beaten up on picket lines,
See the cops commit the crimes.
Move on twenty years then since,
To now give honours to the prince.

Did we change like the green fields,
Burning when the O zone thins and peels.
I woke one day with irony,
To see the people marching free.

Freedom is an easy expression,
Mandela would teach us this lesson.
Of histories truth declared in unity,
That breaks the chains for liberty.

From Soweto to the Orgreave coke works,
Cracking skulls to deny our worth.
Coppers smiling through their overtime,
Smashing skulls their well paid crime.

I'm a victim of this retro hate,
I cashed my giro way too late.
Drinking on saint giro's day,
In the warmth of a July sunray.

Flying

The clear, cold certainty of your expression,
shining intensley through the mists of invention.
Gliding higher still over the rolling green hillsides,
soaring and soaring through a glistening rainbow.
With an abundance of love in the seeds that our faith grows.
Into the winds of fresh newness that carry the fine pearly
clear raindrops, that will nourish our evermore flourishing
passion.
Till we conquer the cloud to require more of our sunshine,
we are flowers in the springtime of our rendevous with the
golden horizon.

In the call of twilights ever clearer conclusion we have found
the secret dreamtime valley. Clothed in velvet green
plushness
of sweet smelling grass vital in the uniqueness of it's
virginity.
We dare not breath of our treasure,
the unspoilt nature in defiance to destruction echoes all our
hatred beneath every rainbow bridges archway.
This valley we have found,
abundant with every diamond coloured proudly shining in
the sun.
Like flowers along a honey milk river bank who see the
golden dew
that speak to us of endless oceans.

We, yes we control the wind surges and the oceans tide of anger,
we raised the mountains that have risen in their yearning to
reach the sky,
the great vast expanse of unchartered decloration vibrating
from every interstella system that promises the storm.
A storm to be the great culmination of mans intensly dumb
depravation of our homeland now scarred and in tatters,
like a battle flag with each tear and hole a badge to the bravery
of headstrong passions or the retreat of cowardice,
or are there neither on the frontline.
Is not every corpse a sales rep to the values of a ceasefire.
Corroded seas grumble and trade winds cough their way
through
heavy times,
I know why cries a voice.
But it has no use the telling of the reason.
They do not hear they speed by so quickly,
they are here one moment and then too far away to plead to,
to barter with that the confrontation is now.
It's either ban the bomb or press the button,
stop the traffic or buy a shotgun.
Let the fox live in peace or accept your condemnation.
The battle lines are drawn by nature,
the tide is turning,
the seas are rising,
the polar ice caps melt away to drown mens destruction,
ignorance and treason to the king who's cause constructs the
balance.

And we teeter and we chant,
and they mock us as they burn the earth.
We will never shrink or fade away from all our trials.
When is it the rainbows turn to win and mans to lose,
can this be a parallel consideration.
Wake up man,
it's like each day a million cars choke me through the fog,
and in my sleep my restless wanderings to dream of
consolidation,
and for this zeal we find a new way till brighter brighter still
we conquer.

Empty Plate

One of the ragged poor,
I'm knocking at your door.
Can you spare some change and bread mister,
I lost everything in Thatchers twister.

I've got no home nor bread tonight,
For me no M.P decides to fight.
I'm a lie to the government I don't exhist,
I will never appear as the rains persist.

One of the ragged poor,
See me begging at the shop front door.
I need some money so I can fly,
On the drug I need to justify.

Oh yea I'm wasted such is disgrace,
Just an addict with broken fate.
I pollute my thoughts with visions of hope,
Smoking realisms ignorance sustained with dope.

I wander streets where with wealth you dine,
The bloated cream from corporate crime.
I cultivate meadows where mushrooms grow,
And protest the bypass in winters glow.

In times begun when from earth I'm gone,
Or earth becomes some forgotten song.
About how the children inherit hate,
Who followed the liars that annialate.

Earth Zero One

Across a vast expanse of reason,
I wake from visions grown out of season.
To wonder why your cache was hoarded,
And why the sycophants applauded.

When deceit became a hunter kill,
Deciding to search for me until.
I arose from chains that held me in the grave,
I looked around for those I shone to save.

When rain came and destroyed the crops we yield,
Flooded valleys drowned one country as a field.
Taxed to forget the lies that sank and drowned or swam,
To eliminate hope and deny the word I am.

Can it be the sun will burn to forever shine,
And melt polar ice to flood the world in time.
That yearns for nutrition of a loving smile,
A rainbows touch not glowing to beguile.

To eastern dreams may love then become,
A heart beating, thudding, burning like the sun.
That never dies but nurtures life that we behold,
Now a commodity of greed only to be sold.

Oh can it be that hope will then decide,
To fly our colours across the mountainside.
And wake the followers of our true desire,
To rise with vengeance like a burning fire.

World Power

Arriving in the dawn the town was still sleeping,
I was nursing my feet from the miles they'd been keeping.
And I took from a step the milk that was left,
then I drank it and yawned for I had not slept.
So I watch the sun rising through my blurry eyes,
and I drift away to wonder if the clouds heavy prize,
will fall in the morning on this day that we meet.

Carrying the burden of love that we saved,
an emotion we sought through the wreckage of the raid.
My heart was becoming a stone in your gaze,
as you defiantly blocked my comments of praise.
What if it was never a blue sky in change?,
what if the sun was unknown and strange?,
and the rain stayed forever and was never betrayed.

Roses are something we rally ourselves to die for,
why is the current state of mind to find much more?.
Appealing to me from the sky flew an angel,
who left me a rainbow and a sweet valley to smell.
With flowers in my eyes painted precicely to cover,
all of my needs in the arms of my lover,
tears of violet in the haze of midsummer.

Arriving in fashion a new age full of romance,
as summers intention shines the sun into a dance.
Onto white water rushing from the soul of a mountain,
in the act of supporting dry fields that are shouting.
For succour and life in the dusty bowl of seclusion,

for the love of pure water during a drought of intrusion,
but a kiss from a cloud brings a brief introduction.

I see through the intense veil of my dreams,
down in the suburbs life's not what it seems.
And we are the fish in the swell of the river,
always imploring much more from the giver.
Whilst we destroy the purity of our souls with the deception,
that it's not for our planet that we seek a correction,
the sun burns and we need some protection.

A carefree dandylion gives it's seeds to the breeze,
when we hurt we are forced by love to our knees.
Describe for me a reasonable belief,
secured in the truth that the wind is a thief.
For before it raced over the fields in the morn',
my eyes were enthralled by the perception of dawn,
my body is weak and the wind is a thorn.

Then it is the ever changing moods of a painter,
it is through disgust that we spit at a traitor.
It is for our passions the reasons we invent,
the excuses for our faults we build through intent.
Now the barricade has been breached as we slept,
and the promises we bought are not being kept,
we know anyway what we like to protect.

Gutters Ode

Can I become my shadow,
Fading away from these pillars aglow.
They hurt my eyes torn up to flinch,
Expanding mire on my clothes to stench.
That saturates me into empty pockets,
Stretching tears from blown eye sockets.
In my pursuit from hunger I,
Intend to berate tears that intensify.
As my heart regains your souvenir,
To speak your name and disappear.

In cities built to create we pray,
Always becoming announced to crave.
The drugs we tempt our limbs to create,
And lessen guilt flowing complete.
Our mind divulge visions of infinity,
To regulate the tides of liberty.
That revolve inside our bleeding minds,
To bring your knees down before the blind.
Has sympathetic tear refused it's cheek,
And made our Sunday roast unique.

The poorest smile at irony,
They write the songs for unity.
Announce your presence in living rhymes,
To benefit and to realise the crimes.
A shadows gleaming frozen tear,
A dead mans cheek can swell it clear.

The rags of forgotten crushed memory,
Inside a staged denounced fraternity.
Where we fall to then revive,
Our lengthy protestations to survive.

Idealism

Unwoven dreams messaged me,
From realms of sleep in sanctity.
When I saw your face through misty cloud,
I called desires awoken sound.

Far into eyes that control liaison's,
Nurtured through summer the elite of seasons.
Becalmed over oceans windless reaches,
Stretched to stun your waves to beaches.

Like empty skies of starless nights,
Searching distances for a guide of lights.
For wander on these endless shores
And lose yourself through sensual force.

Again we reach your rainbow camp,
Like foxes wretched skulk of tramp.
To forage hope through hunters field,
A rightful quest for blood congealed.

Into days where sunshine speeds,
To grow the tangled spread of weeds.
That's grown too tall amongst the crop,
Right to the cliffs of century drop.

Calculate raindrops to fill your bowl,
Unleaded, pure, determined, whole.
Cleansed for futures dealt surrealism,
Saved anointed to create idealism.

Liberty Hangs

When reality requests illusion,
in a saddened state of true collusion.
I dream of divinities drowned resolve,
around the sun where we revolve.
To encounter peace within each smile,
burning all and sundries mile.
Whenever choice becomes illiterate,
we voice to ears all the degenerate.
Because matter burns again the voice,
to undermine what we will rejoice.
Down alleyways of turgid mourn,
blessed without that feeling scorned.
Be it lost in eternal suns,
marching to those rebel drums.
Into battle born for blood,
shining smiling eyes from far above.
In holyness that peels the word,
to gain at first and then at third.
Coining emptiness to touch,
beholding tears shed too much.
Before each captain kills the king,
to end the obscure suffering.
In misty valleys feigning hope,
strung out on some marxist dope.
To free the people sipping wine,
for the beat of cuckoos chime.
That awaken heroes for the score,
and bleed some reason all the more.
Then dying voices choke on anger,
and liberty well they hang her.

Frozen Passion

Oh in this heart is pain,
like a thousand daggers from loves assassin.
Masked and furious in serial necessity,
unchecked and marauding through my life.
I find sleep in hatred,
love turned sour becoming flames of remorse.
The winter growls like bears awoken,
hunting lovers mercilessly.
In a nightmare of distinguished cruelty,
waking sweat soaked calling her name.
No soothing voice nor tender kiss,
distraught and panting as panic attacks.
Lonliness grasping at my throat,
choking me, the life from my heart whimpers away.
Stale tears call on rejuvination,
I fall to the floor broken and lost.
Where is the light in this doomed expanse?,
swimming in darkness crying incoherently.
Come back to me and rescue my soul,
this winter night even freezes passion.

Wet Dreaming in the Sun

Somehow the shaft of blue electric light found corners of the
darkened room that have never witnessed the sun,
and I am running into walls of steel.
Trapped inside the collapse of another kiss,
thinking is this feeling always real.
The levitation of my soul came with rolling laughter,
designed to set my mind at rest,
but without the balance that ate my fear I would have failed
the test.
All around me now I see an arrangement of sunflowers,
I am reaching out to own their colour.
I need this tameing feeling given by the smell,
as I have much time to cover.
Then and only when time allowed me to raise the strength to
leave the room I walked free into the street.
Suddenly the earth glowed brightly and the fragrance of
the flower,
told me that the time had bowed to my freedom in this hour.
Everything was passing onward toward a destination,
that I had never chartered once with this new expectation.
Arriving at the tree I found,
not one not two but twenty pound.
Looking inside a circular tube made of shiny steel,
I ask myself just one more time if I should make a deal.
Calmed and influencing statues to dream,
as they stand quiet still to watch the scene.
I sit upon a stretch of grass green and freshly vital,
and searching my mind to find a word I begin a new recital.

Strange shapes governed the landscape,
each one dictating influence in my search to find escape.
But diamond mines swept images into my mind,
all sorts of dazzling colours form rainbows of every kind.
And I wallow in expensive fantasies,
of even owning natures breeze.
Flying into the ever blue,
I thought a lot, much more of you.
And far away inside my brain,
I hear the colours call my name.
As my rhyme changes from slow to fast,
I chase the dream that glided past.
But when I caught the vision and swallowed up I was,
things arrived to greet me and left me no because.
So free now and yawning I am wrapped up in fluffy cloud,
and seeing into passions eyes it was my love she found.
Pouting kisses search my body and touch says I am the one,
for then a voice encouraged love to join us in the fun.
Slowly I am awakened from a time that slept inside,
and the dream it swam to someone new upon the morning tide.

Kangaroo Babylon 1990

Thought deep within myself turns it's head once more,
politically woven with an old political score.
To lose once more just one more time,
to bow down to those shoes we shine.
Would be the ultimate to the sell out brigade,
who use our votes in a democratic charade.
With eyes blind folded and laces tied in knots,
led by the nose to the crocodile shops.
And all the while we see the deceivers,
leading a pack of profit margin dope dealers.
Taking away those liberties,
with the rise of inflation,
and a wages freeze.

We will rise,
we will rise.
From the dirt of the profit that we opitomize.
Where is your pride,
in this bitter sweet democracy you can never hide.
I have tried.

Leading the demonstration we see the whole street erupt,
I'm scared and run for cover I feel a boot corrupt.
My breath is coming shorter in the panic of the hooves,
and glares of light breaks through the sweat,
who proves,
the cavalry to be or not to be who screwed the questions,
in the censors dingy cupboard whilst we all sat watching
westerns.

It seems though not me after television pictures as I'm brewing
up some tea.
Thats why I take three sugars in this bitter sweet democracy.

Lightning Source UK Ltd.
Milton Keynes UK
UKHW042337041119
352883UK00001B/4/P